MW00761386

Can You Paint a Picture With Your Hair?

Even MORE words, poems and
drawings by
Jeff Whitcher

Copyright © 2015 by Jeff Whitcher

All rights reserved. No part of this publication may be reproduced, distributed, or transmitted in any form or by any means, including photocopying, recording, or other electronic or mechanical methods, without the prior written permission of the publisher, except in the case of brief quotations embodied in critical reviews and certain other noncommercial uses permitted by copyright law. You may contact the author at Whitcherjeff@yahoo.com

To my parents

Free Ride

I wouldn't ride a buffalo,
no telling where he'd want to go.
I wouldn't ride a platypus,
I think that she'd get mad at us.
I wouldn't ride a kangaroo,
and I suspect you wouldn't, too.
I wouldn't ride upon a moose,
for fear the saddle might come loose.
I wouldn't ride a polar bear,
It's much too cold for me up there.
I wouldn't ride an alligator,
even if you paid me later
Would I dare ride an antelope?
Of course the answer would be, nope.
I wouldn't want to ride a bison,
I don't care if it's a nice one.
I wouldn't ride a pelican,
his mouth would open, I'd fall in.
I wouldn't ride a giant whale,
I get too seasick when I sail.
Call me unadventurous,
I think that I'll just take the bus.

Hug for Sale

I'll give you a hug
but I'm charging a nickel.
For just fifteen cents
I can give you a tickle.
A quarter will buy you
a friendly handshake,
and for a high-five
a whole dollar I'll take.
I guess no one here can
afford my small fee.
All right, then,
I guess you can have them for free.

Lemonade stand

Will you buy my lemonade?
This cold refreshing batch I made?
I ran out of lemons
and couldn't find sugar.
My brother, I think,
might have dropped in a booger.
It isn't quite yellow,
It smells kind of fishy.
There's things floating in it,
that feel pretty squishy.
The water is cloudy,
but quite safe to drink,
(though I can't guarantee
that it came from our sink.)
Will you buy my lemonade?
I won't try some, I'm too afraid!

My Mother Made Me Eat a Worm

My mother made me eat a worm,
what kind of mom does that?
The worm was dirty, pink and squirmy,
juicy, long and fat.
I didn't want to eat the worm,
I turned my head away.
I told my mom I didn't have
much appetite today.
My mother said "You'll eat this worm,
now not another word!"
I think I'd like to be something,
anything,
other than a bird.

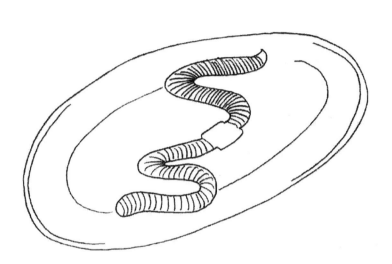

Barbara the Barber

I'm Barbara the Barber extraordinaire.
I love to do wonderful things to your hair!
I only cut hair with my favorite shears.
They haven't been sharpened in 25 years.
When I'm done just be thankful you still have both ears.
I'm Barbara the Barber extraordinaire.

I'm Barbara the Barber extraordinaire
When I'm finished I guarantee people will stare!
The right side I buzzed and the left side I cut,
the color is purple with polka dots but,
it doesn't look bad if you keep your eyes shut.
I'm Barbara the Barber extraordinaire

I'm Barbara the Barber extraordinaire
I specialize in hairstyles no one else will wear.
I hope with your haircut you won't be appalled
You know what my favorite hair style is called?
Bald!

Head Stand

I finally learned how to
stand on my head,
I practiced it for weeks.
And that is why I have these
tennis shoe prints on my cheeks.

My Aunts

Please don't make me visit aunt Ruth!
Please don't make me visit aunt Ruth!
She has hair on her chin and only one tooth,
she thinks she's discovered the fountain of youth,
and gets really mad if you tell her the truth.
Please don't make me visit aunt Ruth!

Please don't make me visit aunt Helen!
Please don't make me visit aunt Helen!
She can't say hello without cursin' and yellin',
how many mice live in her house there's no tellin',
for lunch she serves up nine month old
watermelon.
Please don't make me visit aunt Helen!

Please don't make me visit aunt Mary!
Please don't make me visit aunt Mary!
She has fifteen cats that are big, mean and scary,
they shed so darn much that her furniture's hairy,
I'd rather go sleep in a dark cemetery.
Please don't make me visit aunt Mary!

Please don't make me visit aunt Betty!
Please don't make me visit aunt Betty!
She gives me bear hugs when her armpits are
sweaty,
her dog turns my comic books into confetti,
she serves raccoon meatballs with frozen spaghetti,
Please don't make me visit aunt Betty!

Please don't make me visit aunt Sue!
Please don't make me visit aunt Sue!
she burps when she talks and she spits when she
chews,
her toenails are so long they poke through her
shoes,
each time we play checkers she makes sure I lose,
Please don't make me visit aunt Sue!

Can You?

Can you floss your teeth with a spiderweb?
Can you tickle a jellyfish?
Can you build a machine to turn your skin green,
or any color you wish?
Can you teach a hamster checkers?
On your elbows can you walk?
Can you pick your nose with just your toes?
Can you eat a piece of chalk?
Can you paint a picture with your hair?
Can you draw a fingerprint?
Can you knit some wool pajamas out of belly
button lint?
Can you pierce the ears of an elephant?
Can you stare down an iguana?
Can *I* do any of these things?
I can, but I don't wanna.

Frankenstein in a Tutu

If you see Frankenstein in a tutu
on a pair of hot pink rollerblades,
in a tall witches hat with a scary black cat
and a pair of dark wraparound shades,
If you spot such a strange exhibition
and your eyes can't believe what they've
seen,
don't get spooked out or stressed,
it's my weird sister dressed
in her costume for next Halloween.

I Ate a Sponge

To win a dare
I took the plunge
and ate a dirty
kitchen sponge.
It tasted gross,
all caked with grunge,
and nearly made my
stomach lunge.
I think my mom
would lose her lunch
if she found out
I ate her sponge.
Do you think it
will look suspicious
if tonight
I lick the dishes?

My Favorite Shirt

Mom won't let me wear this shirt,
she says it's gross and reeks.
I told her that's because it ain't been
washed in seven weeks.
It may have holes and greasy stains,
and yes, some sweat marks it contains,
but so far only *she* complains.
It's still my very favorite shirt,
no matter ripped or smeared with dirt.
Perhaps a washing wouldn't hurt….
But does it *have* to be today?
Mom says she means it.
That's okay.
It didn't fit right anyway.

Hat

I'm selling a hat owned by
Abraham Lincoln,
I still don't have a buyer.
I'm not sure if I'm a lousy salesman,
or just a terrible liar?

Cold Toes

My toes were cold
so to warm them up
I put them in my ear.
They wouldn't all fit
and on top of it,
I couldn't really hear.
Instead I put them in my mouth,
five toes inside each cheek.
They all got wet
and worse still yet,
I found I couldn't speak.
I thought I'd put them in my nose,
that didn't turn out well.
There was room for just two,
(which is eight toes too few)
and besides I couldn't smell.
I put them underneath my arms
since both armpits were free,
but that was wrong
'cause all night long
they kept on tickling me.

And then I had the bright idea
to put them in my hair.
But try as I might
I gave up the fight,
they wouldn't reach up there.
So I guess that my feet
will just have to be cold
from my ankles right down to the soles.
I think that my toes
would be so much warmer
if my socks weren't full of holes.

Pass it

Pass the pepper,
Pass the salt,
Spilled the sugar?
It's my fault.
Pass the ketchup
and grated cheese,
Pass the mashed potatoes please!
Pass the butter
and pass the bread,
Pass the knife so I can spread.
Pass the veggies,
Pass the rice.
(Please don't make me ask you twice.)
Pass the....oops!
Excuse that sound.
Hey, where you going?
Sit back down!
Boy, this room sure
cleared out fast.
I guess it was
my turn to pass.

Hammer Time

My father has a hammer
but he doesn't hammer nails.
He pounds his fingers and his thumbs,
then curses, sobs and wails.
My mother says it's all his fault,
he's stubborn as molasses.
He wouldn't have a banged-up hand
if he would wear his glasses.

Read or Read?

Read or read?
Read or read?
It's confusing, guaranteed.
Read or read?
Read or read?
I'm not sure which one I said.
Read or read?
Read or read?
It depends which one you need.
Lead or lead?
Lead or lead?
I give up, I'm going to bed.

The Toy Box Ate My Parents

I told you before
not to go through that door,
or you'd suffer a terrible fate.
I warned mom and dad
that the toy box was bad,
but I guess they just heard me too late.

I yelled out, "Beware!
but my folks didn't care
that a toy box was lying in wait.
They opened the door
and it crawled 'cross the floor,
and my dear, loving parents it ate.

So now it's just me
left in my family,
because nobody heeded my warning.
You should far away get,
'cause I'm willing to bet
he'll be hungry again in the morning.

My Shadow

I was going to do my chores today,
going to sweep and mop the floors today,
even clean out all my drawers today,
but my shadow said, "Let's not."

I was going to wake up at dawn today,
and mow both the front and back lawn today,
but my shadow knew that you'd be gone today,
and he lazily said, "Let's not."

I was going to finish my math today,
even going to get into the bath today,
but I chose a much different path today,
because my shadow said, "Let's not."

So a valuable lesson I learned today,
since a week of no T.V I earned today,
my advice so that YOU don't get burned today,
is to just tell your shadow to HUSH!

New Eyeballs

I need some new eyeballs,
mine turn into cryballs
whenever my feelings are hurt.
Instead of these cry ones
I need some good dry ones,
the kind that won't drip on my shirt.
I really would prize
having waterproof eyes,
that have never one single tear shed.
Give me brown, hazel, blue
any color will do,
just as long as they never turn red.

Secret

I tried to keep a secret
but it sure enough got free.
I only wish I'd known how hard
to keep it safe would be.
It slipped out very sneakily
when I was not aware,
I turned around and suddenly
the secret wasn't there.
I tried to run right after it
as quickly as I could,
but learned that once a secret's gone
a secret's gone for good.
And now I'm sad 'cause ever since
that secret ran off free,
it seems nobody's interested
in sharing theirs with me.

Photo Booth

I went inside a photo booth,
it messed my hair
and pulled my tooth,
even though I made it a dollar richer.
It poked my eyes
and tickled my chin,
and pinched me
when I tried to grin,
if you don't believe me just look at the
picture!

Stink Feet

People tell me my feet stink,
they gag and point and wheeze.
They say my feet are smellier
than rotten, moldy cheese.
I've never, ever washed my feet
nor wiped them with a towel,
they scare the bravest mice away,
so must be pretty foul.
To know that I have stinky feet
does not give me the blues,
because it means that nobody
will ever steal my shoes.

Emergency!

There's a dinosaur in our backyard!
A pirate stole mom's credit card!
I think I saw a ghost downstairs!
Our kitchen's been invaded by bears!
A spaceship landed on our roof,
I'll take a picture if you want proof!
My arms and legs are turning green!
The cat just drank some gasoline!
A gorilla drove away in our car!
I found a rat in the cookie jar!
The baby's downstairs trying to shave!
The dog threw up in the microwave!
Sister caught a squirrel and wants to
boil it!
I dropped dad's wallet in the toilet!
I'm running out of stories to make up
trying to get my parents to wake up.

Bed Jumping

Fred was jumping on the bed
while giggling and squealing.
He bounced so high that me oh my,
he went right through the ceiling.
Fred continued leaping
on his mattress like a goof,
then oh my word, that silly bird
went crashing through the roof!
That crazy Fred kept hopping
and by now had drawn a crowd,
they watched him soar with every bounce
as high as any cloud.
I'm not quite sure how far he got
I'd have to do the math.
He could have kept on going
but an airplane crossed his path.

The Amazingly Fearless Invincible Mike

The Amazingly Fearless Invincible Mike
liked to jump things on his motor bike.
First popped a wheelie when he was a tyke,
The Amazingly Fearless Invincible Mike.

The Amazingly Fearless Invincible Mike,
lined up twelve busses all painted alike,
twenty-four hay bales, two miles of barbed wire,
seventeen barrels, eight cows and a choir,
lastly a circus tent held down with spikes.
The Amazingly Fearless Invincible Mike.

The Amazingly Fearless Invincible Mike
started to rev up his old motor cyke.
A large crowd had gathered they chuckled and cheered,
believing that crazy old fool would get smeared.
But Mike wasn't bothered, he stared straight ahead,
and hitting the gas up the tall ramp he sped.
"You folks can go right on and laugh if you like,"
said fearless Amazing Invincible Mike.

The Amazingly Fearless Invincible Mike
flew through the air, but a bus he did strike.
Crashed through the bales and the barrels and barbed wire,
took out the cows and wiped out half the choir.
Flattened the circus tent, started a fire,
Thought to himself, "If I'd only jumped higher."
Broke every bone in his poor body twice
did Fearless Amazing Invincible Mike.

The Amazingly Fearless Invincible Mike
now much prefers a red three-wheel trike.

Hiding Place

I hid inside my school back pack,
I thought I was clever indeed.
I wouldn't have to go to class,
do arithmetic, writing or read.
It is a fact that this back pack
was not such a smart place to hide.
I have to pee but I can't get free,
'cause the zipper is on the outside.

Cliff Notes

I'm clinging here to the edge of this cliff
by one poor, solitary lone finger.
I'm so tired and weak,
I can hardly speak.
I'm not sure how much more I can linger.
I've been hanging so long,
I no longer feel strong,
from my head right on down to my britches.
With my arm almost numb,
 I fear no help will come,
and oh boy, how that one finger itches!

Rattlesnake Belt

My uncle bought a rattlesnake belt
for a dollar thirty-five.
He met a sad fate,
'cause he found out too late
that the snake was still alive!

Long Necked Larry

I wish I had the neck of a giraffe,
But probably quite a few people would
laugh…..
Okay, what if the size was half?

Toenail Collection

Would you care to take inspection
of my rare toe nail collection?
There are twenty or so
from my big toe,
and fifty or more
from the other four.
I can't believe how many I've got,
some are mine and some are not.
A few are long and others smallish,
some have red and blue nail polish.
A couple are yellow,
a couple are cracked,
some have a nasty fungus, in fact.
I'll let you keep one,
take your pick.
Why do you look like you're going to
be sick?

Yellow Dandelion

Yellow dandelion,
growing tall and straight,
people say you're just a weed,
but I think that you're great.
Yellow dandelion,
standing there so proud,
even with so many friends
you stand out from the crowd.
Yellow dandelion,
you're my favorite flower.
Glowing in the midday sun
above the grass you tower.
Yellow dandelion,
amid this lawn of clover.
I have to say goodbye for now
'cause here comes daddy's mower.

You Can't Do That

"You can't do that," they always say.
"Don't try it, little man."
I go and do it anyway,
to show them that I CAN.
"Don't even dream of doing this,"
(they tell me that a lot.)
But I set out to prove I CAN,
when they say I CAN NOT.
"You simply MUST NOT!" people cry,
"This foolishness must cease!"
I guess they *were* right after all
'cause here come the police!

Upset Stomach

My stomach was grumbling,
it pouted and whined
and said, "Don't you think
 it's about time we dined?"
I said "Stop your griping,
you're acting so rude.
It seems all you ever can
think of is food!"

"I'm sorry for moaning
and acting so crummy,
but how 'bout a snack?"
begged my poor hungry tummy.
"It's two in the morning,"
I said with a yawn.
"I'll give you a bite
when it's closer to dawn."
My stomach grew angry
and let out a growl
to show it was not going
to throw in the towel.
"I can't wait that long
and I won't!" said my belly,
"Just feed me some cookies
or toast with grape jelly.
A nice grilled cheese sandwich,
some soup or a scone,
a quick bite or two
and I'll leave you alone.
There's leftover pizza
 if I'm not mistaken,
now hurry before both
your parents awaken!"
Not wanting to hear
any more of his pleading
I tiptoed downstairs
for some nocturnal feeding.
I emptied the fridge
and the cupboards and shelves,

my stomach and I
made a pig of ourselves.
We ate for a solid
two hours at least
and had the most
wonderful, glorious feast.
I cleaned up the mess
and behind left no trace,
remembering even to
wipe off my face.
I closed all the cupboards
and pushed in the chairs,
then turned off the light
and crept back up the stairs.
But just as the stairs
I began to go up
my stomach said ,
"Uh oh, I have to throw up."

Pumpkinhead Paul

Pumpkinhead Paul had a bowling ball,
but needed some money and sold it.
The next time he bowled,
(so the story is told)
he just took off his head and rolled it.

Leftover Poem

I wrote this verse with leftover words
I had lying around my home,
I picked up some letters and mashed
them together,
and what do you know? A Poem!
So what you are reading
is simply repeating
used adjectives, verbs and nouns.
It just goes to prove you can make
something new,
from old things you have lying around.

The Best Singer Ever

Would you like to hear me sing?
I'm sure of course you would.
In spite of what some people say,
I think I'm pretty good.
Regardless of which song I choose,
I sing extremely well.
Though sometimes people might confuse
my singing for a yell.
I'm very good at opera,
and jazz and rock and pop,
but sometimes I have trouble
knowing when it's time to stop.
My parents say they love my voice,
of course they both are proud.
It's just that they'd prefer it
if I didn't sing so LOUD.

The Spider

Said a mother spider to her frightened son,
"What are you crying for?"
The trembling spider softly said,
"There's a human on the floor."

The mother spider shushed her son,
"This nonsense you must quit.
It's just as much afraid of you
as you're afraid of it."
Young spider stopped his whimpering,
"You think that's really true?"
His mother nodded with a smile,
"Of course, my son, I do."
She gave her son a clever wink,
"Now do just as I say.
Go scurry 'cross your ceiling quick
and *he* will run away!"

The Challenger

I want to play a game of tag
But nobody will chase me
I want to run a half mile dash
But nobody will race me
I want to have a boxing match
But nobody will fight
I'll settle for an arm wrestle
But nobody will bite
I want to play a game of chess
But no one pays me mind
I'd even go for checkers
But no takers can I find
I think it's 'cause they're
'fraid I'll win
that no one makes a peep,
Or maybe 'cause it's 3a.m
and everyone's asleep?

Nose Bubbles

Polly put chewing gum
into her nose,
because she was curious to see
when she blows,
if bubbles would come out

of both nostril holes.
Turns out when a chewing gum
nose bubble grows,
and gets so enormous
it finally explodes,

a boogery chewing gum
nose bubble goes
all over your face
and all over your clothes,
all over your hair
and all over your toes,
all over the carpet,
the couch and windows.
And as it so happens
she also now knows,
just how bad a tantrum
her angry mom throws.
She won't be
blowing bubbles
for a long while
I suppose.

Staring Contest

If you ever should dare
to challenge a bear
to a contest of who can stare longer,
don't think for a minute
you're going to win it,
because, friend, you couldn't be
wronger.
I think that you'll find
what is on the bear's mind,
is not whether he'll come out the
winner.
The bear doesn't care
who the longest can stare,
he's just sizing you up for his dinner!

Horn

Why does a rhinoceros have a horn
if his mouth cannot reach it to blow?
I bet if you asked the rhinoceros
even he probably doesn't quite know.
He may not have ever considered
this fine instrument that he has.
And yet all the same,
I believe it's a shame
that we never will hear him play jazz.

Dad's Waffle

I put some syrup on dad's waffle,
but he yelled, "This sure tastes awful!"
He gagged and tried
to scrape it off
when I told him the flavor was
cherry cough.

No Hugs For Me

I've never, ever in my life
a single warm hug had.
I wonder why it is folks think that
hugging me is bad?
I stand here waiting patiently
my arms stretched out so wide,
I've wished and hoped that someone would,
but no one's even tried.
Would you mind giving me a hug?
I sure could use the practice.
I ought to say that by the way
I am a giant cactus.

Somebody Broke a Window

Somebody broke a window,
our neighbor is upset.
Somebody broke a window,
he doesn't know who yet.
Somebody broke a window,
but no one will confess.
Somebody broke a window,
it's anybody's guess.
Somebody broke a window,
the vandal must be caught.
Somebody broke a window,
to pay for it, he ought.
Somebody broke a window,
there's a round hole and a crack.
I'll tell him who I think it is
if he'll give me my ball back.

There's a Meatloaf on Your Head

It must have been ten years ago
that I first heard it said,
"Excuse me, sir, but did you know,
there's a meatloaf on your head?"

I never knew quite what to say,
my face would turn bright red,
each time someone would mention,
"There's a meatloaf on your head."
Among the folks that I would meet
it seemed a common thread,
"I hate to stare, but are you aware
there's a meatloaf on your head?"
I traveled lands both near and far,
and word would always spread.
"Pardon me, but there seems to be
a meatloaf on your head."
I'm not embarrassed anymore,
and feel no urge to hide,
I do not care who notices,
I hold my head with pride.
I actually have grown to like
this hunk of meat I wear,
I only wish I knew
exactly how it got up there?

Hot Dog

Hot dog!
Hot dog!
Eat a lot dog!
One right now would hit the spot dog!
Hand me one right off the grilly,
with some relish, mustard, chili!
Hot dog!
Hot dog!
Glad I got dog!
Begged for one and daddy bought dog!
Glory, glory hallelujah,
I can't wait to bite into you!

Oops, it fell and hit the floor.
I don't want it anymore.

Play Time

Played checkers with some cucumbers,
Played marbles with some peas,
Played hockey with some celery sticks,
Played dominoes with cheese,
Played soccer with some cantaloupe,
Played frisbee with some bread,
Played football with a pineapple,
Slam dunked a lettuce head.
I find these games enjoyable,
perhaps a little crude.
But mother sent me up to bed,
for playing with my food.

One Last Poem

There's one last poem hiding here
somewhere,
I'll be darned if misplaced it.
It was clever and witty,
and therefore, a pity
if we had to go and waste it.
I think it's somewhere in this book,
will you help me look around it?
It should be right here,
but I can't see to clear.
Oh wait, I think you found it!

Other books by this author you will absolutely love:

What If Balloons Didn't Pop?
Words, poems and drawings by Jeff Whitcher
What If Balloons Didn't Pop? is the first collection of humorous poems and drawings by Jeff Whitcher. Guaranteed to make kids and adults of all ages giggle, Whitcher's silly Shel Silverstein-inspired poetry covers everything from fish in space to hide-and-seek playing giraffes!

The Incredible Story of the (Not-so) Amazing Genie of the Lamp
A story in words and pictures
The second book by author and illustrator Jeff Whitcher, this lighthearted tale of a mysterious genie who appears to a young boy (and gives him slightly less than he bargained for!) will give children and adults of all ages a serious case of the giggles!

Have You Ever Heard A Goldfish Burp?
More Words, poems and drawings by Jeff Whitcher
This collection of delightfully offbeat and silly poems and drawings from the mind of Jeff Whitcher will engage and entertain kids (and grown-ups) of all ages. Even if you've never heard a goldfish burp, watched an elephant mow the lawn or crossed paths with a bad-mannered tooth fairy, this book will have you rolling with laughter!

The Alphabet Book

Explore the wonderful world of ABCs with this charming and hilariously whimsical journey through the alphabet. From guitar-playing elephants to tap-dancing tooth fairies this book will tickle the funny bones of young and old readers alike!

(Almost) Everything Poops

(Almost) Everything Poops is a refreshingly unconventional and humorous take on one of the earliest and most important life lessons taught to children. Geared toward the pre-preschool crowd, this interactive and delightfully simple book is part educational, part comical and 100% silly!

34473613R00054

Made in the USA
San Bernardino, CA
29 May 2016